"Sahana Vij believes that food can foster bonds among people, that baking is a path to understanding the lives of others, and that through cooking she can improve the world she lives in. She backs up her beliefs with action, donating her proceeds from *Bake Away* to No Kid Hungry. This young baker gives me hope for the future."

–THOMAS KELLER, CHEF & PROPRIETOR, THE FRENCH LAUNDRY

"Sahana brings her own blend of innovation and artistry to each recipe in *Bake Away*. She takes us on a journey, demonstrating on each page and with every experience that baking fosters community. Through charitable donations Sahana shows her love to give, reinforcing our faith that food has the power to help others."

–HUNTER LEWIS, EDITOR-IN-CHIEF, *FOOD & WINE*

"What a treat to hear Sahana's stories through her words and experiences. If there was a space in the sibling baking club, I would most certainly have jumped in line. From Atlanta to Temescal Valley, molten lava cake to cinnamon bagels, you won't be able to choose where to start your journey in *Bake Away*. My suggestion is to start at page one and live the book, page by page, until you reach Sahana enlightenment!"

–TOM DOUGLAS, CHEF & OWNER, TOM DOUGLAS SEATTLE KITCHEN

"I am so impressed with Sahana's thoughtful approach to developing recipes and the sense of place she imbues in her creations. The road trip she's created through her fun dishes is inspiring and creative."

–SONIA CHOPRA, EXECUTIVE EDITOR, *BON APPÉTIT*

"Food has always been a language of love, and the act of breaking bread together creates more than just memories, but also communities. *Bake Away* shares this vision of using food as a bridge and a literal lifeline to help those in need. Sahana's culinary journey is vibrant, dynamic, diverse, and delicious! Her passion and philanthropic spirit shines through her desserts. You'll enjoy cooking through this book, one sweet bite at a time!"

–JUDY JOO, RESTAURATEUR & TV CHEF ON FOOD NETWORK AND THE COOKING CHANNEL

"It is so encouraging to see a young person like Sahana following her dreams by writing this inspired cookbook and committing to her convictions by donating her royalties to No Kid Hungry. Her recipes are diverse, playful, and absolutely delicious. Sahana has taken this opportunity to remind us of the deeper reason cooking is a central part of our lives: creating connections and making memories with the people we love."

–LUDO LEFEBVRE, CHEF & OWNER, PETIT TROIS

"Reading each recipe took me on a culinary journey with Sahana, and I will be using this amazing cookbook in my kitchen for years to come! I feel a bond with Sahana through a shared influence of travel that inspires our baking, and her dedication to making the world a better place makes her a hero among us!"

–BRIAN HART HOFFMAN, EDITOR-IN-CHIEF, *BAKE FROM SCRATCH*

"Taking inspiration from childhood memories, family travels, and beloved recipes, Sahana has put together an inspired cookbook that leaves me feeling excited about the next generation of passionate cooks."

–ANGELO A. SOSA, CHEF & RESTAURATEUR

"Sahana and her recipes are inspiring, adventurous, and full of gratitude. *Bake Away* is a clever collection of work for a heartfelt cause."

–CANDICE KUMAI, CHEF & BESTSELLING AUTHOR

"*Bake Away* is fun and inspiring. Sahana's recipes are inviting and approachable for any baker, and she enhances them by weaving in stories from her childhood along the way. Best of all, she's publishing this book to support a very important cause, No Kid Hungry."

–TARA DUGGAN, ASSISTANT FOOD EDITOR, *SAN FRANCISCO CHRONICLE*

BAKE AWAY

www.mascotbooks.com

Bake Away: Twenty Recipes Capturing the Spirit of Creativity, Experience, and Expression

Food photography by Sahana Vij

Location Photography by:

Page 4: iStock.com/Ron and Patty Thomas; Page 8: iStock.com/july7th; Page 12: iStock.com/deberarr; Page 18: iStock.com/Juliana Vilas Boas; Page 26: iStock.com/YinYang; Page 30: iStock.com/graphiknation; Page 36: iStock.com/BCFC; Page 40: iStock.com/simonkr; Page 44: iStock.com/BWiatre; Page 48: iStock.com/njsciple; Page 52: iStock.com/doug4537; Page 56: iStock.com/4nadia; Page 62: iStock.com/pdpetersonphoto; Page 66: iStock.com/pkphotography; Page 70: iStock.com/Ahorica; Page 76: iStock.com/wingmar; Page 80: iStock.com/DianeBentleyRaymond; Page 86: iStock.com/alacatr; Page 90: iStock.com/tiny-al

For more information, please contact:

Mascot Books
620 Herndon Parkway, Suite 320
Herndon, VA 20170
info@mascotbooks.com

Library of Congress Control Number: 2020918115
ISBN-13: 978-1-64543-645-4
Printed in the United States

www.bakeaway.com

Jostens is proud to fund all printing and production expenses of *Bake Away* to maximize donations made to No Kid Hungry.

For over 125 years, Jostens has inspired millions of students like Sahana to pursue their passions and to celebrate their achievements. For more information on Jostens products and programs supporting students and schools, visit Jostens.com and jostensrenaissance.com.

To my family
and beloved,
Niko 🐾

BAKE AWAY is a celebration of baking's impact on our creativity, self-expression, and personal experiences. It's a reflection of what's important in our lives.

From the delicate Portland Berry Cream Pie to the towering Atlanta Crêpe Cake, Sahana Vij brings you on her journey of inspiration, sharing the simple steps to create an array of delightful desserts, each crafted from personal connections and beautiful memories. Each recipe is accompanied by exquisite food photography and portraits of stunning locations.

Explore an elegant fruit garden in Temescal Valley as you make a luscious Citrus Poppy Seed Bread. Learn a little about Maui as you prepare a decadent Coconut Chocolate Tart. Share a subtly spiced Chai-Infused Cake, inspired by visits to a prominent tearoom in Seattle, with those you love. *Bake Away* is more than a cookbook: it is a beautifully written book grounded in family, relationships, and giving.

BAKE AWAY

TWENTY RECIPES CAPTURING THE SPIRIT
OF CREATIVITY, EXPERIENCE, AND EXPRESSION

— SAHANA VIJ —

CONTENTS

INTRODUCTION

I was five years old when my mom taught me how to make garlic bread. She was about to cook dinner — pan-fried chicken, grilled vegetables, and a garlic bread appetizer. I leaped up on my step stool, eager and excited to watch, but this time I wanted to actually *help*. I was only in first grade, and I thought I was ready to be the sous chef; I was ready to chop the vegetables and pan-fry the chicken. My mom, of course, did not want me to cut or burn myself, so she decided to give me a safer job, preparing the appetizer. I was slightly disappointed; nonetheless, I agreed. Grabbing the pre-sliced baguette, my mom began setting the slices on a metal baking pan lined with tinfoil. She melted some butter and grabbed a small bottle of Italian seasoning, demonstrating how to spread the butter and sprinkle the seasoning over a slice of bread. My mom handed me the spoon and walked back toward the stove, leaving me to follow her instructions.

Ambition and excitement flooded my mind as an opportunity of my own presented itself, motivating me to impress and try my best. I spread the butter, captivated as my eyes followed the gleaming golden substance blanketing the slice. Sprinkling the seasoning was like watching glitter fall from my hand, each particle discovering a spot on which to lie along the butter. Despite my mind's enchantment, I was inexperienced in the kitchen, and my hand grew tired by the weight of the spoon. My mom returned, and she noticed I had put too much butter and a little too much seasoning; she suggested I try again. After a few more tries, I was delighted by not only experiencing such a fascinating task but to have made a dish I could share with my family. I peered through the oven's window, observing the slices glow to a golden brown. After arranging them on a serving dish, I placed the appetizer on the table. That excitement and new love for cooking was met with my newfound ability to share and bring joy to others. I watched as, one by one, a new slice was swept from the dish and added to a dinner plate. The process is what thrilled me, each methodical step had a meditative and entrancing element.

My excitement for cooking never left, and it soon transitioned into a love for baking. I began watching videos and studying cookbooks when I was six years old, learning how to create delectable blueberry muffins and strawberry macarons. These cookbooks guided me into the world of baking, teaching me how to perfectly whip egg whites and knead dough, just as my mom taught me to evenly spread the butter and sprinkle the Italian seasoning. I used these guides as stepping stones, learning to master foundational baking recipes and challenging myself with new and unknown recipes. I flipped through pages and pages of recipes, unlocking new flavors and discovering advanced techniques. Soon, I whipped up strawberry cakes, apple pies, banana breads, and fudge cookies, sharing them with my family and friends. Watching my mom tear up at the sight of the lavender cake I made her one Mother's Day and my dad's joy while biting into the bite-size apple pies I made for Thanksgiving is what continues to inspire me.

Almost every summer, I visit my cousins in Atlanta. We spend most of our time outdoors, escaping the heat and cooling down in the pool. One afternoon after swimming, I decided to make a New York blueberry cheesecake. I asked my cousins, who were draped in towels and dripping water on the floor, if they wanted to join. My younger cousin gave an emphatic *Yes!* It took some more convincing, but we eventually rounded up the other two. After drying off, we all met back up in the kitchen and grabbed the ingredients. My younger cousin measured the sugar and the flour, while the oldest and I combined the cream cheese, sugar, and butter in a stand mixer. We found a springform pan and finally placed the cake and pan in a water bath in the oven. After the long process and hard work, we sat waiting for the timer to go off. Right at the beep, we whipped open the oven and stared at our finished creation, excited to take the first bite. We began to decorate the cheesecake as our aunts and uncles took pictures and our other two cousins eagerly came to taste the creation. We watched as each forkful of cake entered a mouth, hopeful our hard work had paid off. Smiles grew across each face; even the youngest cousin who was only two years old motioned for seconds. We were all relieved, thankful none of us happened to mix up the salt and sugar. Now, whenever I visit them, we take cooking to the next level, having baking and gingerbread house competitions, and creating new Christmas dinner recipes.

Baking has allowed me to express my creativity, bond with others, and bring joy to those around me. I have also been able to infuse my experiences into what I bake, using flavors and ingredients that symbolize special memories. Focusing on the recipe and techniques does yield exceptional results, but the true prize of baking comes when I share those exceptional results with others.

Each of the twenty recipes in this book represents a key defining moment that has shaped me into the person I am today. Each one incorporates a part of myself, my family, and most importantly the strong *connection* cooking and baking has built between me and my loved ones. Each recipe includes where it was created, with whom, and why it is important to me. From visiting cousins in Atlanta to grandparents in Temescal Valley, I focused on a few simple recipes that have made a difference in my life. Baking has offered me a way to understand and connect with others. I wanted to share that, transform it into a language that we all understand, and contribute what I have learned.

A large aspect of this book is grounded in family, relationships, and giving. I want you to pick up this book, try out a recipe or two, and hopefully feel a connection to a person or beautiful memory from your life.

SAHANA VIJ

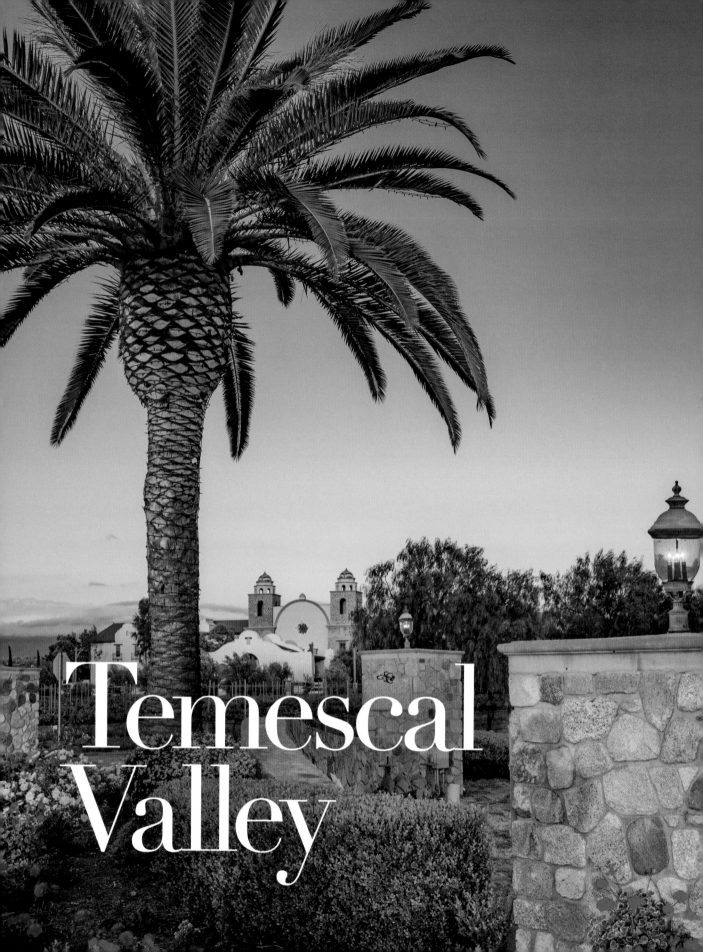

Temescal Valley

INSPIRATION

This recipe was inspired by visits to my grandparents' home in Temescal Valley, California. My grandparents love their garden where they grow a wide variety of fruits including pomegranates, figs, guavas, and lemons. The garden played such a special role in my childhood that I wanted to dedicate a recipe to it. My grandparents taught me how to spot when fruits were ready for picking, and showed me creative ways to use them in dishes. Lemon bread perfectly captures the essence of these adventures, but traditional lemon bread was a little too plain. Adding poppy seeds and glaze elevates the bread and adds wonderful flavor.

TEMESCAL VALLEY CITRUS POPPY SEED BREAD

YIELD: 1 9 X 5-INCH LOAF

TIME: 2 HOURS

INGREDIENTS

BREAD

1 Tbsp safflower or vegetable oil

1 egg

1 Tbsp vanilla extract

⅓ cup granulated sugar

½ cup Greek yogurt

Zest and juice of 1 lemon, separated

2 cups flour

2 Tbsp poppy seeds

½ tsp baking powder

½ tsp baking soda

⅛ tsp salt

⅓ cup milk or almond milk

GLAZE

½ cup powdered sugar

¾ tsp vanilla extract

3 tsp milk

DIRECTIONS

1. Preheat oven to 350°F.

2. Butter a 9 x 5-inch bread loaf pan.

3. In a large bowl, combine the oil, egg, vanilla, sugar, yogurt, and lemon juice.

4. In a separate medium-sized bowl, combine the flour, poppy seeds, lemon zest, baking powder, baking soda, and salt.

5. Begin alternating between adding the dry mixture and milk to the wet mixture until fully added and combined.

6. Once completely combined, pour the batter into prepared bread dish and bake in oven for 30 minutes. Allow to cool in pan for 1 hour.

7. While bread is cooling, prepare the glaze. In a small bowl mix the powdered sugar, vanilla, and milk until smooth.

8. Once the bread is completely cooled, drizzle the glaze over bread with a spoon. Slice and serve or store in refrigerator for up to 3 days.

Seattle

INSPIRATION

Chocolate molten lava cakes have been my favorite dessert since I was three years old. Whenever my parents took me out to dinner, I ordered a chocolate molten lava cake at the end of the meal. Growing up in Seattle, Fran's Chocolates, Seattle Chocolate Company, and Theo Chocolate were extremely popular. My obsession with molten lava cakes paired with all the chocolate brands I grew up around inspired me to create an inviting chocolate molten lava cake dedicated to Seattle, Washington.

SEATTLE MOLTEN CHOCOLATE LAVA CAKES

YIELD: 6 LAVA CAKES

TIME: 30 MINUTES

INGREDIENTS

6 Tbsp butter

½ cup semisweet chocolate chips

¾ cup powdered sugar

2 eggs

2 egg yolks

1 tsp vanilla extract

½ cup flour

DIRECTIONS

1. Preheat oven to 425°F.

2. Butter 6 custard cups and place them on a baking sheet.

3. Microwave the butter and chocolate chips in a large bowl for 1 minute, then mix thoroughly until chocolate chips are fully melted.

4. Stir the sugar, eggs, egg yolks, and vanilla into the chocolate mixture until fully combined. Then stir in the flour.

5. Pour the batter evenly into the 6 custard cups. Bake for around 10 minutes, or until sides of the cake are firm but the interior is still soft.

6. Allow the cakes to cool for a couple minutes, then place a plate over the custard cup and flip the chocolate cake over onto the plate. Be sure to use an oven mitt in case the cups are still hot. Serve immediately.

Try these Seattle Molten Chocolate Lava Cakes with SoHo Salted Caramel Ice Cream (page 14).

SoHo

INSPIRATION

While visiting New York, my dad and I dined out at the first pizza parlor in America. After devouring our dinner, we were eager to discover the desserts of SoHo. We came across an ice cream shop that offered a variety of nuanced flavors, but we were both drawn to the caramel ice cream. This recipe is my best attempt at recreating the ice cream we both loved in SoHo. I absolutely love this ice cream, and it goes wonderfully atop the Seattle Molten Chocolate Lava Cakes (page 10).

SOHO SALTED CARAMEL ICE CREAM

YIELD: 1 LITER

TIME: 1 HOUR PREPARATION, 1 DAY TO FREEZE

INGREDIENTS

ICE CREAM

1 cup heavy cream
2 cups milk
1 tsp vanilla extract
½ cup granulated sugar
3 egg yolks

CARAMEL

¾ cup granulated sugar
5 Tbsp butter, softened
¼ cup heavy cream
1 tsp coarse salt

DIRECTIONS

1. To make the ice cream base, heat the cream, milk, and vanilla in a large pot on medium heat until the mixture is warm to the touch.

2. In a small bowl, whisk the sugar and egg yolks until combined.

3. To temper the yolks, add ½ cup of the warm cream mixture from Step 1 to the egg mixture. Whisk together until fully combined.

4. Add the mixture from Step 3 back to the large pot with the remaining cream. Stir over medium heat until the back of a spoon inserted is fully coated. Remove the pot from heat and allow to cool.

5. While the mixture is cooling, prepare the caramel. Pour the sugar into a medium saucepan. Continuously stir the sugar over medium-high heat until the sugar is completely melted, roughly 5–7 minutes.

6. Lower the temperature to medium-low. Slice the butter into individual tablespoons and add them one at a time to the saucepan while continuously stirring to fully combine. Be careful—the mixture will bubble due to differences in butter temperature and heated sugar.

Directions to be continued on page 16

SOHO SALTED CARAMEL ICE CREAM
(CONTINUED)

DIRECTIONS

7. Slowly pour the heavy cream into the sugar-butter mixture while stirring constantly until fully combined.

8. Whisk in the salt and set caramel aside to cool and thicken for about 5 minutes.

9. After caramel has thickened, pour the caramel into the ice cream base while whisking fast and continuously to prevent the two portions from separating, until fully combined. It should result in an even medium-brown color.

10. Pour caramel ice cream mixture into an 8 x 4-inch metal pan. Freeze uncovered for 24 hours.

11. Once frozen, scoop ice cream and serve.

New York

INSPIRATION

Drawing on inspiration from my trips to New York with my dad, I immediately knew I had to include a recipe for a great New York-style bagel. I decided it needed a twist, or should I say, a *swirl*. These New York Cinnamon Sugar Bagels are a bit different than the typical plain or everything bagel served with cream cheese. I thought it would be fun to mix the sweet and sugary aspects of New York—all the candy stores and ice cream sundaes—with the classic New York breakfast of a bagel and coffee. Then, to top it off, I added some sweetness to the staple cream cheese spread to create a delicious cream cheese frosting.

NEW YORK CINNAMON SUGAR BAGELS WITH CREAM CHEESE FROSTING

YIELD: 8 BAGELS

TIME: 3 HOURS 30 MINUTES

INGREDIENTS

BAGEL

1 ½ cups warm water

¼ oz active dry yeast

½ cup granulated sugar

3 ½ cups flour

1 ½ tsp cinnamon

1 tsp salt

1 tsp vanilla

CINNAMON SUGAR SWIRL

2 Tbsp granulated sugar

1 ½ tsp cinnamon

WATER BATH

8 cups water

¼ cup honey

EGG WASH

2 egg whites

1 Tbsp water

CREAM CHEESE FROSTING

8 oz cream cheese

5 Tbsp softened butter

1 ¼ cups powdered sugar

1 tsp vanilla extract

DIRECTIONS

1. Preheat oven to 425°F and line two baking sheets with parchment paper.

2. To make the bagels, pour water then the yeast into the bowl of a stand mixer fitted with a dough hook attachment. Allow to sit for 2 minutes, then mix on medium-low speed for 1 minute. Cover with plastic wrap and let sit for 5 more minutes.

3. Add the sugar, flour, cinnamon, salt, and vanilla to the bowl. Using the dough hook attachment, beat the mixture on low for about 2 minutes until dough is firm and a bit dry.

4. Move dough onto a lightly floured surface, and knead it with your hands for about 5 minutes, or until it is soft and bounces back to your touch.

5. Place dough in a lightly greased bowl, cover the bowl with a kitchen cloth, and allow dough to rise for 1 hour, or until it doubles in size and is at room temperature.

6. While the dough rises, mix the cinnamon and sugar in a small bowl for the cinnamon sugar swirl.

Directions to be continued on page 22

NEW YORK CINNAMON SUGAR BAGELS WITH CREAM CHEESE FROSTING
(CONTINUED)

DIRECTIONS

7. Once the dough is finished rising, move the dough onto a lightly floured surface and use your hands to press dough into the shape of an 8 x 12-inch rectangle. Sprinkle the cinnamon sugar mixture over the rectangle evenly, and gently press it into the dough.

8. Fold the rectangle in half and cut the dough into eight even strips.

9. Gently shape each folded piece into a ball, while trying to keep the cinnamon sugar swirl inside the ball.

10. After balls are formed, press your finger through the center of each ball, and press outward to create a hole in the center. Shape the dough out until the center of the bagel is about 1 inch wide and the whole bagel has a 5-inch diameter. Leave finished bagels off to the side on a floured surface.

11. In a large pot, prepare the hot water bath by whisking together the water and honey. Bring the water to a boil, then place 2 bagels at a time into the water bath. Allow 1 side of the bagels to cook for 1 minute, then flip with a fork and allow the other side to boil for an additional minute. Place the finished bagels on a large plate.

Directions to be continued on page 24

NEW YORK CINNAMON SUGAR BAGELS WITH CREAM CHEESE FROSTING
(CONTINUED)

DIRECTIONS

12. To prepare the egg wash, whisk together the egg whites and water in a small bowl. Brush the tops of each bagel with the egg wash.

13. Place bagels on the prepared baking sheets and bake for 15–18 minutes, or until bagels are golden brown. Remove the bagels from the oven and place them on a wire rack to cool for 30 minutes.

14. While the bagels are cooling, prepare the frosting. Whip together the cream cheese, butter, sugar, and vanilla in the bowl of a stand mixer fitted with a wire whisk attachment. Mix on medium speed for 3–5 minutes, or until a thick, creamy mixture forms.

15. Once the bagels are room temperature, slice them in half and toast, if desired. Spread cream cheese frosting on bagels and serve immediately.

Kauai

INSPIRATION

Family trips to Kauai were always the highlight of my summers. My cousins and I absolutely loved the tropical atmosphere, especially the food. During one visit, we toured an enormous garden and tasted the varieties of fruit it produced. The guide chopped up mangoes and pineapples, among other fruits, to share. The mango tasted different from the ones I had gotten back in Seattle—they were sweeter. The pineapple was fresher with a bit more tang. I have always appreciated that experience and wanted to turn one of my favorite fruits into a dessert. A smoothie felt refreshing and an enjoyable treat for the heat.

KAUAI TROPICAL SMOOTHIE

YIELD: 2 SERVINGS

TIME: 10 MINUTES

INGREDIENTS

1 lb frozen strawberries, mangoes, and pineapple medley

1 cup milk or milk alternative

2 ripe bananas

DIRECTIONS

1. Place the frozen fruit, milk, and bananas in a blender.

2. Blend ingredients for about 1–2 minutes, or until smooth. You may need to mix with a spoon every 30 seconds to blend out chunks.

3. Pour the smoothie into two glasses and serve immediately.

Atlanta

INSPIRATION

On my visits to Atlanta, my younger cousin and I are usually the first to wake up every morning. We are always eager to plan the menu for breakfast before everyone wakes up; my cousin's first choice is consistently crêpes. Usually, I begin making the batter as I ask him to slice the strawberries and bananas. When both of those are done, we work together to make the chocolate sauce. We spread the sauce, add the fruit, and fold the crêpe, topping it with powdered sugar. I wanted to capture this memory by transforming the crêpes into a cake. For this recipe, I included the base ingredients from our favorite sweet breakfast dish.

ATLANTA CRÊPE CAKE

YIELD: 1 9-INCH CAKE

TIME: 1 HOUR 30 MINUTES

INGREDIENTS

CRÊPES

1 ½ cups milk

4 eggs

4 Tbsp melted unsalted butter

2 Tbsp granulated sugar

¼ tsp salt

1 cup all-purpose flour

WHIPPED CREAM FROSTING

1 cup heavy cream

2 Tbsp granulated sugar

1 tsp vanilla extract

Fresh berries for topping

DIRECTIONS

1. Place the milk, eggs, and butter in a bowl. Whisk until ingredients are fully combined and the mixture resembles a smooth, yellow, creamy liquid. Add in the sugar, salt, and flour and whisk until a smooth, watery batter forms.

2. Heat a nonstick 10-inch pan over medium heat. Melt a thin pad of butter in the pan and coat the surface using a spatula.

3. Scoop ¼ cup of the batter into the center of the pan. Pick up the pan so it is slightly above the stove top and turn the pan in a circular motion until the batter coats the entire bottom of the pan. Make sure to spread the batter along the edges to create an even circle and an evenly spread surface.

4. Rest the pan back over the heat and let the crêpe cook until it is set. Make sure there is no loose, wet batter surrounding or covering the crêpe.

5. Gently push the spatula under the edges of the crêpe, ensuring the crêpe can be flipped and is set. Flip the crêpe over and let it cook for a few seconds.

6. You can now transfer the crêpe onto a plate to allow it to cool to room temperature.

Directions to be continued on page 34

ATLANTA CRÊPE CAKE (CONTINUED)

DIRECTIONS

7. Continue making crêpes until the rest of the batter is made, and lay the rest out to cool.

8. To make the whipped cream frosting, blend the cream, sugar, and vanilla in a stand mixer fitted with a whisk attachment. Whisk ingredients for roughly 5–7 minutes, or until frosting holds peaks.

9. To assemble the cake, begin by placing a crêpe on a cake dish and then spread about ¼ cup of the whipped cream frosting over the crêpe until an even layer is spread. Continue stacking the crêpes and spreading frosting until the cake is roughly 7–8 inches tall. There may be extra crêpes and frosting, but don't continue stacking them above 8 inches, otherwise the cake may become unsteady and easily tip.

10. Coat the top of the cake with whipped cream frosting and leave the sides bare. Top with fresh berries, slice, and serve.

Phoenix

INSPIRATION

One year, my grandparents and I flew down to Phoenix, Arizona, to visit my cousins. One evening during the trip, my dad went out to the grocery store and brought back a bag full of avocados. My grandmother began calling us over to the kitchen, prepping us for a demonstration. She carefully took each avocado, peeled the skin off, and motioned for us to do the same. We began doing as she asked while she chopped up onions, tomatoes, and cilantro. When we finished, she placed the avocados in a large bowl and showed us how to mash them. When finished, we added in the tomatoes, cilantro, and onion, as well as the lemon juice and salt. This guacamole recipe was our go-to as we grew up, and we continued replicating it years after. I wanted to create a sweeter recipe with the same fruit. These popsicles are a sweet and cool alternative to the classic use of an avocado.

PHOENIX AVOCADO POPSICLES

YIELD: 10 POPSICLES

TIME: 10 MINUTES PREPARATION, 5 HOURS TO FREEZE

INGREDIENTS

2 ripe avocados, pitted and peeled

14 oz coconut milk, unsweetened

1 cup granulated sugar

DIRECTIONS

1. In a food processor, pulse the avocados, milk, and sugar until smooth and fully combined, about 30 seconds.

2. Fill a popsicle mold with the avocado mixture until full and stick popsicle sticks in the center of each compartment.

3. Freeze for 5–6 hours or overnight. When ready to enjoy, hold the molds under hot water for about 10 seconds and pop the popsicle out and serve immediately.

Los Angeles

INSPIRATION

My dad, uncle, and I visit Los Angeles often, up to two to three times a year. We frequently visit Disneyland where the sidewalks are filled with a sweet, mouthwatering churro smell. Almost every visitor I see on these trips is holding a golden churro with sparkles of cinnamon and sugar left along the edges of their lips. The feeling of biting into a churro while visiting Disneyland was the inspiration I had for this recipe. I didn't want to pursue the classic route of deep-frying, so I decided to opt for a tasty waffle option. The waffle's shape perfectly holds the cinnamon and sugar, and beautifully exemplifies the churro.

LOS ANGELES WAFFLE IRON COOKIES

YIELD: 12–16 MINIATURE WAFFLES

TIME: 30 MINUTES

INGREDIENTS

WAFFLES

2 cups all-purpose flour

¼ tsp salt

1 Tbsp baking powder

1 ½ cups milk

2 eggs

⅓ cup butter, melted

1 ½ tsp vanilla extract

CINNAMON SUGAR TOPPING

4 Tbsp butter

½ cup sugar

1 ½ tsp cinnamon

DIRECTIONS

1. Preheat a square waffle iron/press to medium.

2. In a medium bowl, combine the flour, salt, and baking powder. Create a crater in the center of the flour mixture with a spoon and add the milk, eggs, butter, and vanilla into the center.

3. Stir to incorporate the wet and dry ingredients together until a smooth batter forms with just a few lumps.

4. Once the waffle iron is heated, spread some butter over the iron and spoon in ¼ cup of the batter into the center of the squares.

5. Close the cover of the waffle press, and allow the waffle to cook until the machine beeps when ready. Remove the waffle from the iron and set aside to cool. Continue making waffles with remaining batter.

6. To create the cinnamon sugar topping, melt the butter in a small bowl. In a separate bowl, stir the sugar and cinnamon together.

7. Brush each waffle with the melted butter on both sides, then cover each in the cinnamon and sugar mixture on both sides; be sure to fully coat them. Once coated, serve immediately.

Maui

INSPIRATION

On a trip to Hawaii, my grandparents, my mom, and I were driving to a pineapple plantation when we came across a coconut shack. We stopped on the side of the road and stepped inside the little hut. The shopkeeper was slicing coconuts over a wooden board directly in front of us. My grandfather asked for a coconut and we all stuck straws inside to taste the coconut milk. I had never tasted anything like it. It didn't taste like the milk I was used to drinking. The coconut milk was watery and had a very subtle taste. This simple tart combines the coconut flavor with the rich taste of chocolate.

MAUI COCONUT CHOCOLATE TART

YIELD: 1 9-INCH TART

COOK TIME: 1 HOUR FOR PREPARATION, 1–2 HOURS TO REFRIGERATE

INGREDIENTS

CRUST
12 graham crackers
6 Tbsp butter

CHOCOLATE FILLING
8 oz can sweetened condensed
    coconut milk
¾ cup dark chocolate chips
½ tsp vanilla extract
Raspberries and sliced bananas
    (optional)

DIRECTIONS

1. Preheat oven to 350°F.

2. For graham cracker crust, pulse graham crackers in a food processer until they resemble coarse crumbs, then transfer to a medium bowl.

3. Melt butter, then pour it over crushed graham crackers. Mix until thicker crumbs begin to form.

4. Pour mixture into a springform pan. Pat down graham crackers until a firm ¼-inch base forms.

5. Bake crust in oven for about 10 minutes, or until the crust is slightly darker.

6. Set aside the crust to cool.

7. To make the chocolate filling, melt the coconut milk in a saucepan over medium heat until small bubbles form along the side. Set the chocolate chips in a heat-tolerant bowl and pour the hot coconut milk over the chocolate chips. Whisk mixture until all clumps are gone, then mix in the vanilla.

8. Pour the chocolate mixture into the graham cracker crust and refrigerate for 1–2 hours. Serve with fresh raspberries or sliced banana for extra flavor.

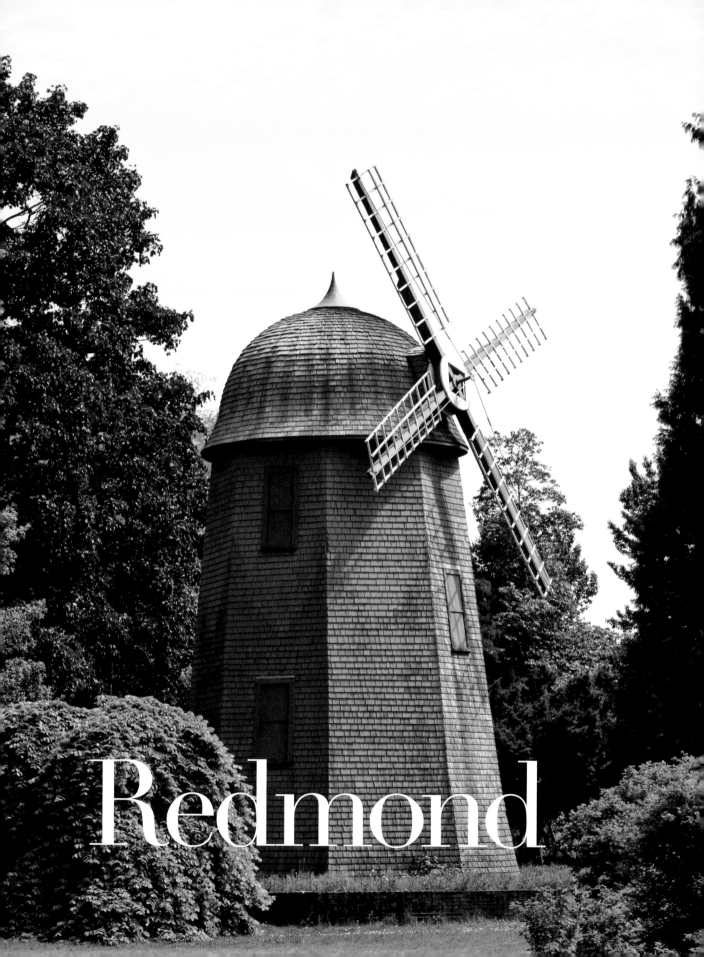

Redmond

INSPIRATION

For this recipe, I was inspired by my hometown. This tart recipe was drawn from my late-night grocery store trips with my mom. We would buy mini fruit tarts filled with custard and savor them once we got home. The tarts had a deliciously delicate vanilla cream filling. I wanted to recreate a similar flavor and capture the feeling of tasting the crème custard. Rather than top it off with berries like the miniature ones at the grocery store, I used a variety of fruits, such as pears, to finish the tart.

REDMOND PEAR CRÈME TART

YIELD: 1 9-INCH TART
COOK TIME: 3 HOURS

INGREDIENTS

CRUST
12 graham crackers
6 Tbsp butter, melted

PASTRY CRÈME FILLING
⅓ cup sugar
¼ cup cornstarch
Sprinkle of salt
1 ¾ cups milk
4 egg yolks
1 Tbsp butter
1 ½ tsp vanilla extract
4 pears, thinly sliced

DIRECTIONS

1. Preheat the oven to 350°F.

2. In a food processor, pulse the graham crackers until they resemble coarse crumbs. Transfer the crushed graham crackers into a medium bowl, add in the butter, and mix together until the mixture begins to form larger crumbs.

3. Pour the mixture into a springform pan and use your hands to press the mixture until a firm ¼-inch base forms.

4. Bake crust for about 10 minutes, or until the crust is slightly darker.

5. To make the filling, in a small bowl combine the sugar, cornstarch, and salt and set aside. In another small bowl, add the milk and whisk in the egg yolks.

6. In a medium saucepan over medium-high heat, melt the butter, add the sugar mixture and the milk-egg mixture, stirring to combine. Heat and whisk the mixture until boiling. Let the mixture boil for around 1 minute, allowing it to thicken. Remove from heat and whisk in vanilla. Allow the filling to cool in refrigerator for 15 minutes.

7. Spoon and evenly spread the chilled filling into the graham cracker crust. Incorporate the pear slices onto the top of the filling, laying them around the exterior working your way inward.

Bloomfield
Hills

INSPIRATION

One summer between my sophomore and junior years of high school, my cousins and I visited my grandparents in Bloomfield Hills, Michigan. We explored photo albums and other treasures to learn more about our parents. One afternoon, my cousin and I were inspired to make a breakfast treat. We grabbed ingredients from our grandparents' pantry and put together this granola. My grandmother, aunt, and I loved it. We ate it almost every day for breakfast with some berries and almond milk.

BLOOMFIELD HILLS GRANOLA

(SUGAR-FREE)

YIELD: 6 SERVINGS

TIME: 45 MINUTES

INGREDIENTS

3 cups oats

¼ cup dried cranberries

¼ cup sunflower seeds

¼ cup shredded coconut

½ tsp cinnamon

1 cup pitted dates

½ cup nut butter

3 Tbsp water

DIRECTIONS

1. Preheat the oven to 350°F.

2. In a large bowl, mix together the oats, cranberries, sunflower seeds, coconut, and cinnamon. Set aside.

3. In a food processor, pulse together the dates, nut butter, and water until a paste with small chunks has formed.

4. Spoon the paste into the oat mixture and use your hands to incorporate the paste into the dry ingredients. Make sure to get all the oats covered by the date and nut paste.

5. Line a baking sheet with parchment paper. Spoon the granola mixture onto the pan, evenly spreading it out to the edges.

6. Bake in the oven for 10–15 minutes. Remove the pan and mix up the granola on the sheet, exposing the parts facing the bottom. Place the pan back in the oven and bake for another 5–10 minutes, or until golden.

7. Let cool for about 30 minutes, then serve with milk or yogurt.

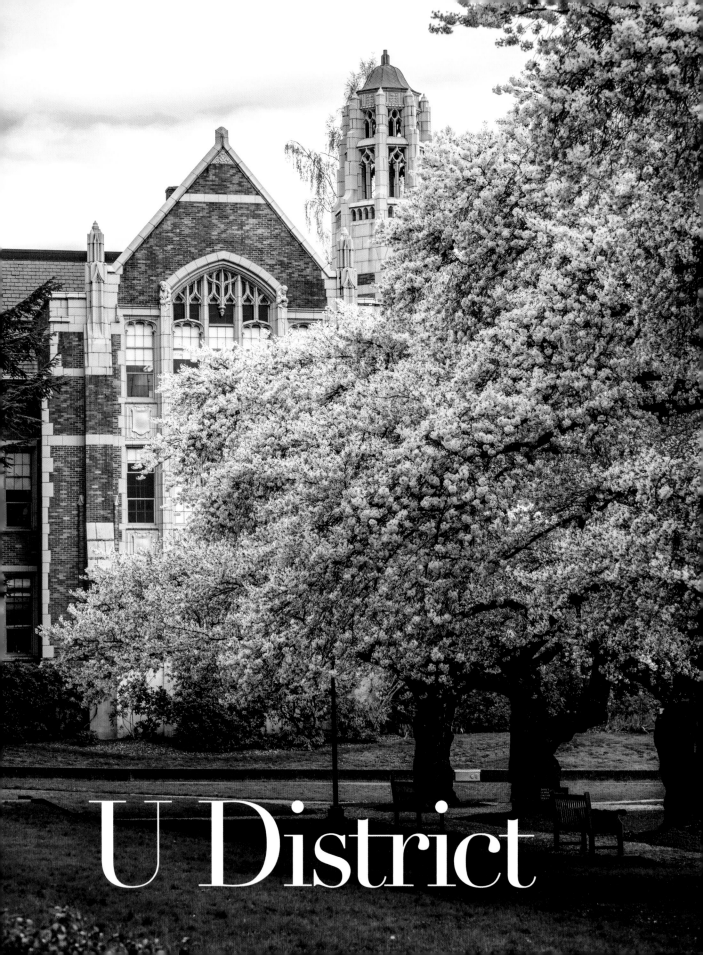

U District

INSPIRATION

Almost every month, my mom and I go to a fun, brightly colored teahouse tucked away on a street in the university district of Seattle. When we walk in, we see a case filled with tarts, pastries, and cakes. A waitress greets us, and she seats us at a table with floral teacups, lace tablecloths, and containers of colored sugar flakes used to flavor tea. We begin looking at our menus, immediately knowing what we will order. We start with a pot of chai. The chai provides just the right amount of sweetness, balancing out our savory meals. This U District Chai-Infused Cake draws from not only the chai from our favorite restaurant, but also from the many pots of chai we brew at home and enjoy together. This cake incorporates the spice-filled flavor of chai topped with a thick and creamy frosting.

U DISTRICT CHAI-INFUSED CAKE

YIELD: 4-LAYER 8-INCH CAKE

TIME: 3 HOURS

INGREDIENTS

CAKE

2 cups whole milk
2 Tbsp chai blend
4 cups flour
1 ½ Tbsp baking powder
1 tsp salt
1 Tbsp cinnamon
2 tsp cardamom
1 cup butter, softened
1 ½ cups granulated sugar
¾ cup brown sugar
6 eggs
2 tsp vanilla extract

FROSTING

8 oz cream cheese
1 cup unsalted butter, softened
1 tsp vanilla extract
5 cups powdered sugar

DIRECTIONS

1. Preheat the oven to 350°F.

2. Heat the milk in a saucepan over medium-high heat for 5–10 minutes or in the microwave for 2 minutes. Using a French press, steep the loose leaf chai blend in the milk for about 10 minutes, then strain and set aside.

3. In a large bowl, combine the flour, baking powder, salt, cinnamon, and cardamom.

4. In the bowl of a stand mixer fitted with the paddle attachment, cream together the butter and sugars on medium-high speed until fluffy. Set the mixer to low-medium and add 1 egg at a time until fully incorporated, then add the vanilla.

5. On low speed, slowly pour in the chai tea to the wet mixture until fully combined. Then slowly pour in the flour mixture, adding 1 cup at a time into the wet mixture. Make sure each addition is fully incorporated before adding the next.

6. Grease four 8-inch cake tins and evenly distribute the batter amongst them. Bake all four for 25–30 minutes, or until a toothpick inserted comes out clean. Flip cake layers onto a cooling rack to cool.

Directions to be continued on page 60

U DISTRICT CHAI-INFUSED CAKE
(CONTINUED)

DIRECTIONS

7. To make the frosting, combine the cream cheese and butter in the bowl of a stand mixer fitted with the whisk attachment on low-medium speed until smooth. Add in the vanilla, then add the powdered sugar 1 cup at a time, making sure each addition is fully incorporated before adding the next.

8. To assemble the cake, slice off the round top on each cake layer so that the top of each layer is even.

9. Place the first layer on a large plate or cake stand, then add about ¼ cup of frosting and spread evenly over the top of the cake. Next, add the second layer and repeat this process until each layer has been stacked. Spread the remaining frosting evenly around the sides of the cake.

10. Top with fruit, flowers, or spices to decorate. Slice and serve.

Scottsdale

INSPIRATION

On one trip to see my cousins in Scottsdale, Arizona, my dad and I bought a s'mores kit from the hotel gift shop. My cousins spent the next day with us at the hotel, swimming during the day and roasting marshmallows over a fire pit in the evening. That night, we indulged in warm roasted marshmallows and chocolate flattened between two graham crackers. These fudge bites combine the same flavors of that night in a new way, with an emphasis on the chocolate.

SCOTTSDALE S'MORES FUDGE

YIELD: 1 6 X 10-INCH BAKING PAN

TIME: 10 MINUTES PREPARATION, 1–2 HOURS TO REFRIGERATE

INGREDIENTS

2 graham crackers

14 oz sweetened condensed milk

3 cups semisweet chocolate chips

½ cup marshmallows

DIRECTIONS

1. Place the graham crackers in a plastic bag, crush the crackers with hands or rolling pin, and set aside.

2. In a saucepan over medium heat, stir together the sweetened condensed milk and chocolate chips until smooth and fully melted.

3. Line a 6 x 10-inch baking dish with parchment paper and pour the chocolate mixture into the prepared dish, smoothing the surface.

4. Sprinkle the graham crackers over the fudge and press the marshmallows into the surface.

5. Refrigerate for 1–2 hours.

6. Allow the fudge to sit outside of the refrigerator for around 5 minutes before serving to easily slice and serve.

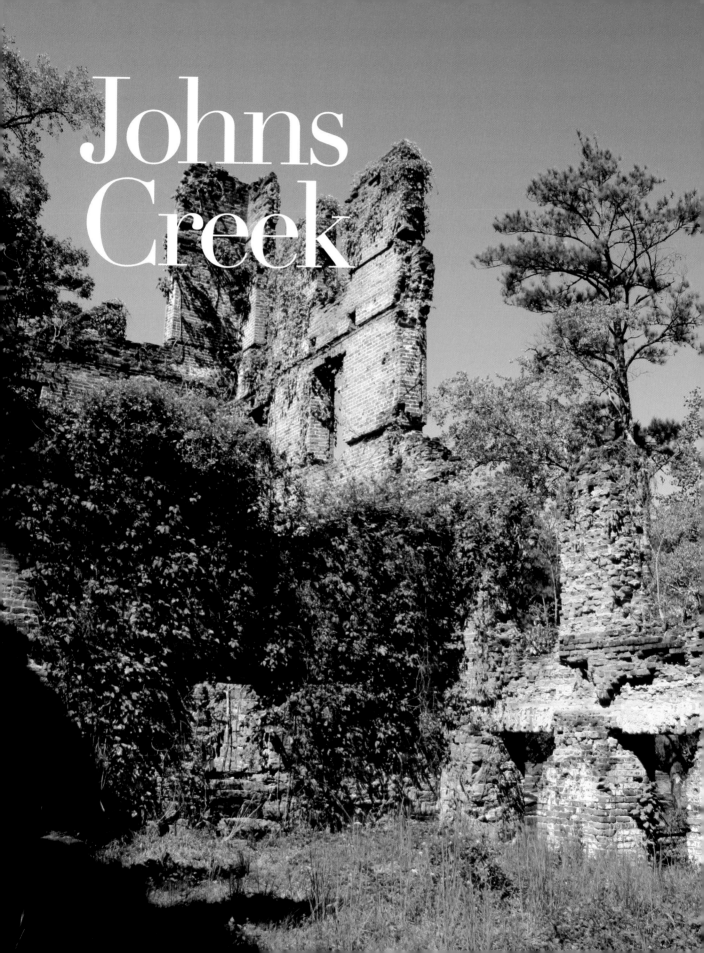

Johns
Creek

INSPIRATION

Large family dinners are a tradition at my cousins' home in Johns Creek, Georgia. My grandparents, aunts, uncles, and a group of cousins gather to eat lasagna, salad, and dessert. Right before dinner, we head to the living room to play with my youngest cousin's toy cars, construct a puzzle, or enjoy a game of Taboo. Our uncle always surprises us with a special dessert from a local bakery. During one particular visit, our ears turned up, listening to the garage door open and hearing his footsteps at the door. We rushed to the kitchen as our eyes found their way to the large box in his arms. He placed it on the counter and lifted the lid, revealing mini red velvet, chocolate, and vanilla cupcakes topped with cream cheese frosting. The chocolate cupcakes are first to go in our family, making them the perfect option to replicate for this recipe. I topped the cupcakes, making a thick, traditional cream cheese frosting.

JOHNS CREEK CHOCOLATE CUPCAKES

YIELD: 12 CUPCAKES

TIME: 50 MINUTES

INGREDIENTS

CUPCAKES

1 cup all-purpose flour

¾ tsp baking powder

½ tsp baking soda

½ cup unsweetened cocoa powder

¼ tsp salt

⅓ cup butter, softened

½ cup granulated white sugar

¼ cup light brown sugar

2 eggs

1 tsp vanilla extract

¾ cup milk

FROSTING

8 oz cream cheese

½ cup butter room temperature

4 cups powdered sugar

Sprinkles (optional)

Pomegranate seeds (optional)

DIRECTIONS

1. Preheat the oven to 350°F and line a 12-cup muffin tin with baking cups.

2. In a medium bowl, combine the flour, baking powder, baking soda, cocoa, and salt. Set aside.

3. In a large bowl, whisk the butter and sugars together until combined. Add the eggs and vanilla.

4. Continue whisking and alternate adding the flour mixture and milk in thirds.

5. Pour about ¼ cup of the batter into each lined baking cup. Bake for 20 minutes, or until a toothpick inserted comes out clean.

6. Take the cupcakes out of the oven and allow to cool for about 15–20 minutes.

7. To prepare the frosting, combine the cream cheese and butter on medium-high speed in a stand mixer fitted with a whisk attachment. Mix for about 30 seconds.

8. Reduce the speed to low and add in the powdered sugar one cup at a time, making sure each cup is fully incorporated before adding the next.

9. Fill a piping bag with the frosting and attach a desired tip. Frost the cupcakes and top with sprinkles and pomegranate seeds, if desired. Serve immediately or store in fridge for up to one week.

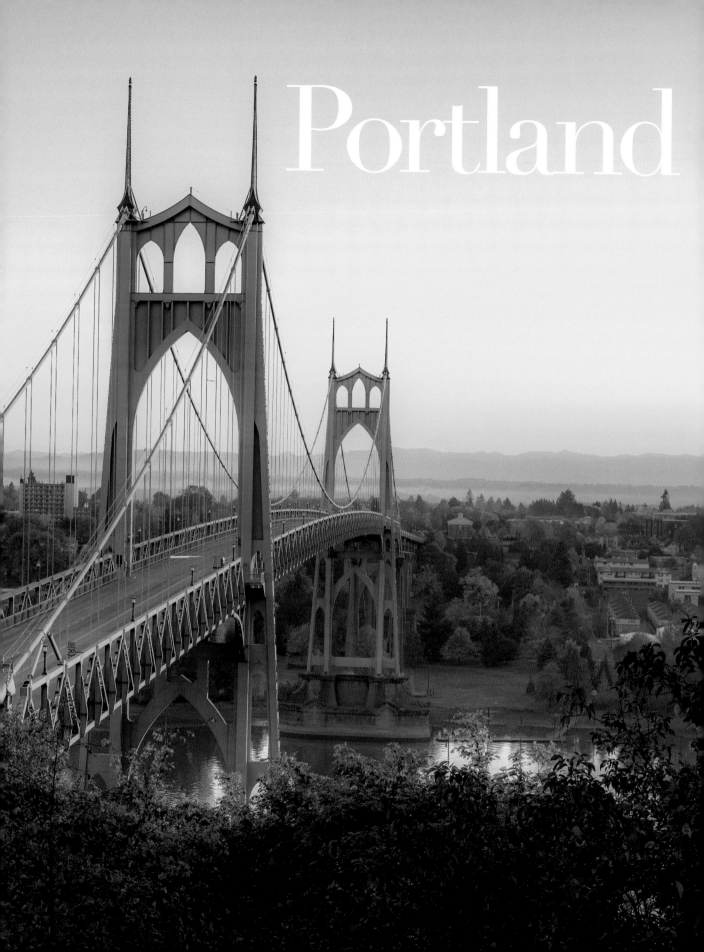

Portland

INSPIRATION

When I was twelve years old, my aunt, cousins, and I took a road trip to Mount Saint Helens and Portland, Oregon. While in Portland, we wanted to learn more about the city, so my aunt signed us up for a biking tour. We biked around the city and crossed the river where our guide stopped us to take a break near wild blackberry bushes. My cousins and I rushed to the bush, eagerly picking the berries and filling our mouths. This recipe incorporates the love my cousins and I had for the fresh berries into a light and creamy pie with hints of vanilla.

PORTLAND BERRY CREAM PIE

YIELD: 1 10-INCH PIE

TIME: 1 HOUR

INGREDIENTS

PIE CRUST

1 ¼ cups flour

1 ½ Tbsp sugar

¼ tsp salt

6 Tbsp cold unsalted butter

¼ cup cold water

CREAM FILLING

½ cup granulated sugar

¼ cup all-purpose flour

⅛ tsp salt

1 ½ cups milk

3 egg yolks, beaten

1 Tbsp butter

1 tsp vanilla extract

WHIPPED TOPPING

1 cup heavy cream

2 Tbsp granulated sugar

1 tsp vanilla extract

Fresh berries for topping

DIRECTIONS

1. Preheat oven to 400°F.

2. To make the crust, blend the flour, sugar, salt, butter, and water in a food processor until dough forms; it should begin to form into one large stiff ball of dough.

3. Remove the dough from the food processor and wrap it in plastic wrap. Refrigerate it for around 30 minutes.

4. Remove the dough from the plastic wrap. Lightly flour a flat, clean surface and roll out the dough with a rolling pin until it is ¼-inch thick. Gently pick up dough sheet and place it in a lightly greased pie pan, pressing it into the shape of the pan.

5. Place a piece of parchment paper over the dough and place pie weights on top of the paper and dough. This will ensure that the crust does not significantly shrink while baking and stays covering the pan.

6. Bake the pie crust for around 15 minutes, or until the crust is golden. Remove the pie crust from the oven and let it cool while you prepare the cream filling.

Directions to be continued on page 74

PORTLAND BERRY CREAM PIE
(CONTINUED)

DIRECTIONS

7. In a saucepan over medium heat, stir together the sugar, flour, salt, and milk. Once the mixture thickens, remove it from heat and add whisked yolks.

8. Continue to cook, stirring continuously until the yolks are fully incorporated. Remove from heat and whisk in the butter and vanilla. Let the mixture cool.

9. Once cooled to room temperature, remove the pie weights and pour filling into baked pie crust. Set aside to make whipped topping.

10. To make the topping, whip the cream, sugar, and vanilla in a stand mixer fitted with the whisk attachment for roughly 5–7 minutes, or until peaks form.

11. Fill the top of the pie with the whipped cream topping, then add sliced fresh berries on top and serve.

Road to
Hana

INSPIRATION

When I was twelve years old, I visited Hawaii with my grandparents and my mom. One morning, we headed out on a six-hour drive on the road to Hana, one of the most popular attractions of Maui for its scenic beauty. This popular winding road made my stomach turn and started up my motion sickness. To combat the stomach pain and nausea, I stared out the window at the overhanging greenery and streams below the road. As we drove, people living along the road began emerging, holding food in their hands. We all had not eaten for what felt like six hours, so we stopped to see what they offered. Almost every single person we met held homemade banana bread prepared with the fresh bananas growing nearby. We purchased some and headed back in the car to drive to Hana. We split up the bread and it held us over until our lunch. The bread was delicious; it was so sweet and moist. Though this recipe has no added sugar, I used extra bananas for a burst of sweetness and natural flavor.

ROAD TO HANA BANANA BREAD

YIELD: 1 9 X 5-INCH LOAF

TIME: 1 HOUR 15 MINUTES

INGREDIENTS

⅓ cup olive oil

2 eggs

4 ripe bananas, mashed

½ cup milk or milk alternative

1 tsp baking soda

1 tsp vanilla extract

¼ tsp salt

1 tsp cinnamon

2 cups all-purpose flour

DIRECTIONS

1. Preheat the oven to 350°F and butter a 9 x 5-inch bread pan.

2. In a large bowl, whisk together the olive oil and eggs, then add the bananas and milk. Mix until fully combined.

3. Whisk in the baking soda, vanilla, salt, and cinnamon. Fold in the flour using a bigger spoon until combined.

4. Pour the batter into the prepared bread pan and bake for 55–65 minutes.

5. Allow to cool for 20 minutes and serve immediately or refrigerate up to one week.

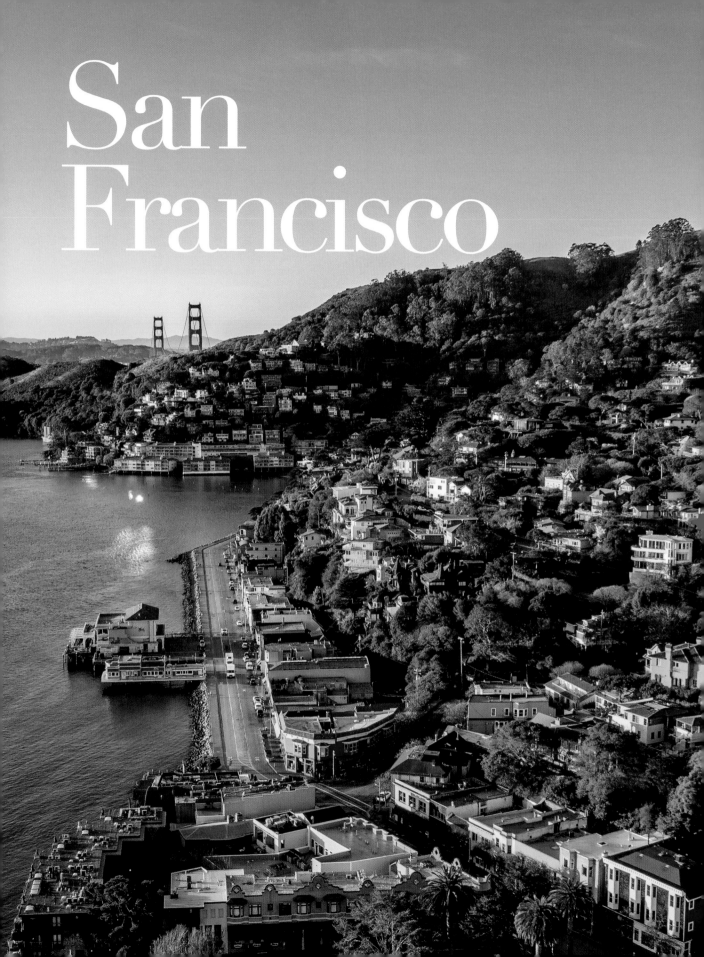

San
Francisco

INSPIRATION

When I was about ten years old, my dad and I met up with his best friend and his wife on a trip to San Francisco, California. We decided to meet at the Ghirardelli Chocolate Factory, learn about how their chocolate is made, and grab a dessert. After the tour, we went to the bakery and ordered a banana split. It was a wide glass bowl filled with Neapolitan ice cream accompanied by a sliced banana and whipped cream, and topped with a maraschino cherry. My face was soon smothered with chocolate ice cream and whipped cream. This recipe draws inspiration from that moment but also adds new flavors to the classic banana split.

SAN FRANCISCO CHURRO BOWLS AND BANANA SUNDAE

YIELD: 6 CHURRO BOWLS

TIME: 1 HOUR PREPARATION, OVERNIGHT TO FREEZE

INGREDIENTS

CHURROS

⅓ cup butter

1 Tbsp brown sugar

1 Tbsp granulated white sugar

½ tsp salt

1 cup water

1 cup flour

1 tsp vanilla

2 eggs

½ cup white sugar for coating

1 ½ tsp cinnamon for coating

2 quarts vegetable oil

CARAMELIZED BANANAS

1 Tbsp butter

1 Tbsp brown sugar

1 banana, sliced

DIRECTIONS

1. In a saucepan over medium-high heat, mix together the butter, sugars, salt, and water until it reaches a boil. Lower the heat to low, then add the flour, folding it in until a dough forms and it is evenly incorporated. Turn off heat and allow to cool for 5 minutes.

2. Once fully cooled, add in the vanilla and eggs, making sure to fully incorporate each.

3. Transfer the dough into a piping bag with a circular or star tip.

4. Flip over a muffin tin and spray the back side with cooking spray to prevent the dough from sticking. Pipe the churro dough around the flipped muffin cups to form a closed-spiral bowl. Freeze the churro bowls for at least 2 hours or overnight.

5. Combine the sugar and cinnamon for coating in a small bowl and set aside.

Directions to be continued on page 84

SAN FRANCISCO CHURRO BOWLS AND BANANA SUNDAE (CONTINUED)

DIRECTIONS

6. Heat the oil in a large pot; the oil should be done heating within 10 minutes. Place the frozen churro bowls in the oil to fry. Allow each to cook for about 30 seconds, then flip to allow each to cook for another 30 seconds, making sure the bowl is a golden brown. Take the churro bowls out and set on a plate with a paper towel to drain.

7. Coat the bowls in the cinnamon sugar mixture, spooning the mixture into the bowls and around the inside of them and making sure to cover them evenly.

8. To prepare the caramelized bananas, melt the butter and sugar in a saucepan over medium heat and add the sliced banana. With a spoon, gently move the banana slices around the pan for about 5 minutes, coating them in the sauce. Turn off stove and move the pan off heat.

9. Scoop store-bought vanilla ice cream into the churro bowls and top with the caramelized banana. Serve immediately.

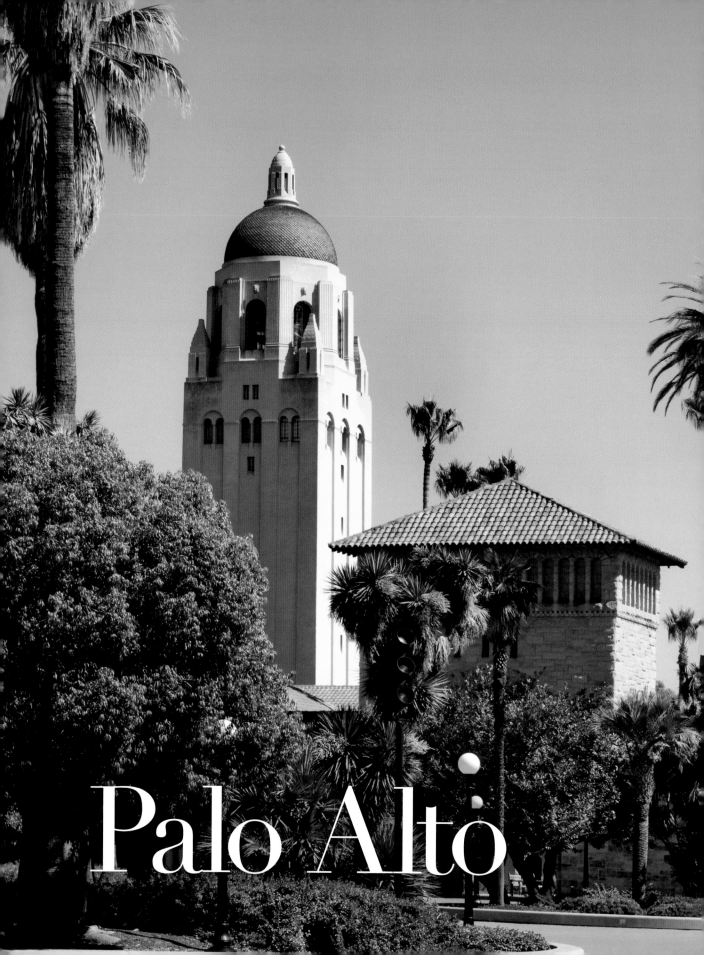

Palo Alto

INSPIRATION

There is an outdoor mall in Palo Alto, California, that my dad has taken me to since I was a baby. A bakery right at the entrance, Cocola Bakery, has always been our favorite place to have breakfast. When I was about ten years old, my dad and I got in line to order our food while I peered inside the glass case, observing the rows of pastries. I carefully made my decision, signaling to my dad that I wanted the Raspberry Danish. Once we finished ordering, I grabbed the treat and headed to the table. We split the Danish in two, and he handed me the bigger piece and enjoyed his smaller one with his espresso. This Danish was my attempt at recreating my favorite pastry in Palo Alto with a fresh raspberry filling and crispy puff pastry layer.

PALO ALTO RASPBERRY DANISH

YIELD: 12 DANISHES

TIME: 45 MINUTES

INGREDIENTS

2 sheets puff pastry

8 oz cream cheese, softened

1 cup powdered sugar

1 tsp vanilla extract

⅓ cup raspberry jam

DIRECTIONS

1. Preheat oven to 400°F.

2. Allow puff pastry sheets to thaw, then roll them out on floured surface.

3. Cut each sheet into 6 rectangles, then place each rectangle on a lined baking sheet. Set aside.

4. In a stand mixer fitted with a paddle attachment, combine the cream cheese, powdered sugar, and vanilla.

5. Spoon about a tablespoon of the cream cheese mixture onto each of the pastry rectangles. Spread out the cream cheese mixture in the center of each rectangle, leaving about ¼ inch of space along the edge of the rectangle.

6. Spoon a teaspoon of jam over the spread cream cheese mixture, creating another layer.

7. Bake in the oven for 15 minutes, or until the puff pastry has risen and is golden. Allow the Danishes to cool for another 15 minutes and serve immediately.

Ann Arbor

INSPIRATION

Over one summer break, my cousins and I took a trip to Michigan to visit our grandparents. One day, we drove to Ann Arbor to walk around the art fair. We passed by tents, searching for a painting for my aunt's new kitchen. Suddenly it started pouring rain. Soaked in water, we ran over to the library and dried off under the hand dryers. When we went back outside, the sun was shining and we were soon fully dried and even started to sweat. Hot and thirsty, my youngest cousin pointed toward a lemonade truck and asked for a cup. We walked over and ordered a few servings. The lemonade delighted us all as we sipped it while strolling and looking at the sculptures and paintings around us. While thinking about how to replicate that refreshing lemonade we had on that scorching day, I felt adding some berries would be a good upgrade. This recipe combines the lemonade we enjoyed at the art fair with flavorful berries.

ANN ARBOR BERRY LEMONADE

YIELD: 6 SERVINGS

TIME: 1 HOUR

INGREDIENTS

10 cups water

1 ½ cups granulated sugar

1 cup raspberries

1 cup blackberries

1 ½ cups fresh-squeezed lemon
  juice (8–10 lemons)

DIRECTIONS

1. In a saucepan over medium heat, combine the water and sugar, stirring until the sugar is dissolved. Remove from the heat and allow to cool.

2. In a blender, blend the raspberries and blackberries until pureed, then press the mixture through a fine mesh sieve, pushing the liquid into a separate bowl. Discard the solid pulp and keep the liquid.

3. In a large pitcher, mix the sugar water, berry liquid, and lemon juice until combined.

4. Add in ice and serve immediately.

In Loving Memory of
My Best Friend, Niko

July 27, 2008 –
September 21, 2020

INSPIRATION

My dog Niko absolutely loved banana and coconut. Every time I baked, he accompanied me, sitting beside me with wide eyes and his ears perked up. He often asked for some leftover ingredients. It would be hours, standing on my feet until whatever creation I had made found its way into the oven, and Niko still sat with me. He would watch from the adjacent room as I opened the oven and set the hot tray on the countertop. That's when he would usually walk over and ask for the finished product. I would slice off pieces for both him and me to try the recipe first, then I would let one of my parents know it was done. As I ate with them, we threw pieces over to Niko for him to catch. Baked goods have always been his favorite, and I wish he could have tried this cake.

Niko, thank you for being my best friend and a brother. I wish you could have tried this cake, and I know you would have sat with me while I baked, wagging your tail for another piece. I miss you buddy, see you soon. I love you, Niko. 🐾

NIKO'S COCONUT CAKE
WITH BANANA FROSTING

YIELD: 4-LAYER 8-INCH CAKE

TIME: 4 HOURS

INGREDIENTS

CAKE

6 cups all-purpose flour

2 Tbsp baking powder

1 tsp baking soda

¼ tsp salt

4 eggs

3 cups granulated sugar

3 sticks butter, room temperature

½ cup vegetable oil

2 Tbsp coconut extract

1 tsp vanilla extract

3 cups canned unsweetened
coconut milk

¼ tsp cream of tartar

FROSTING

1 banana mashed

2 sticks butter, room temperature

5 cups powdered sugar

2 bananas, thinly sliced

1 cup shredded unsweetened
coconut

DIRECTIONS

1. Preheat the oven to 350°F and grease four 8-inch round cake pans.

2. In a large bowl, combine the flour, baking powder, baking soda, and salt, then set aside.

3. Separate the egg whites and yolks into two separate bowls.

4. In the bowl of a stand mixer fitted with the paddle attachment, combine the sugar, butter, and oil on medium speed until smooth. Add in and combine the egg yolks, coconut extract, and vanilla extract.

5. Add in the coconut milk and flour mixture in three additions, alternating between each and making sure each addition is fully combined before adding the next.

6. In a separate small bowl, mix the egg whites with cream of tartar on high speed until they hold soft peaks.

7. Fold in the egg white mixture to the batter.

8. Evenly distribute the batter among the four prepared cake pans and bake for 20–25 minutes.

Directions to be continued on page 98

NIKO'S COCONUT CAKE
WITH BANANA FROSTING (CONTINUED)

DIRECTIONS

9. Allow cakes to cool in pans for about 5 minutes, then proceed to transfer them to cooling racks to continue to cool for an additional 30 minutes.

10. While cakes cool, prepare frosting in the bowl of a stand mixer fitted with the whisk attachment. Combine the mashed banana with butter on medium speed until smooth. Reduce the speed to medium-low and continue to mix while adding 1 cup of powdered sugar at a time, waiting to add the next until the previous one is fully incorporated.

11. Begin assembling cake by placing the first layer of cake on a cake platter or desired serving dish. Spread about ⅓ cup of frosting over the cake and evenly place some of the banana slices over the frosting. Sprinkle ⅓ cup of the shredded coconut over the banana, then place the next cake layer on top of the coconut. Continue adding frosting, layering the banana, and sprinkling the coconut for the remaining cake layers.

12. Once the fourth layer is placed on top, take the remaining frosting and evenly frost the top of the cake and the sides. The frosting along the sides will most likely be a thin layer, and that is okay; the sides of the cake should peer through and the frosting should not coat a thick layer around the cake.

13. Decorate the top of the cake with some extra banana, coconut, or maybe some flowers. Slice and serve.

ABOUT THE AUTHOR

Sahana Vij is a recent high school graduate from the Pacific Northwest. Her passions include swimming, painting scenery with watercolors, and creating memorable desserts for her family and friends. From the early age of four, she has always loved to bake, and her parents (who are both avid cooks) are her inspiration. Spending time with them in the kitchen got her acquainted with simple techniques, and her curiosity led her to expand her horizons into baking. She hungered to learn new baking skills, and her constant practice grew into a passion and love for the activity.

As she visited her family around the country, her experiences influenced and inspired recipes, many of which are included in this book. Sahana developed a deep appreciation for baking as she experienced not only the bonding it fostered with those around her, but the impact she had on others by sharing her creations. Her desire to help others is reflected through this cookbook, as 100 percent of her net proceeds will be donated to help fight child hunger. Sahana hopes she can share her experiences and love for baking with others and with that, help children in need.

ACKNOWLEDGMENTS

Bake Away would have never been accomplished without the support of my family.

I want to thank both of my parents who have supported me on this journey. They have always instilled in me the importance of perseverance, creativity, and compassion, all of which are reflected throughout this cookbook. I also want to thank my extended family, including my aunts, uncles, grandparents, cousins, and my dog for sharing the beautiful memories that have inspired me to create each recipe in this book.

Finally, I want to thank all of the chefs and food editors that have supported *Bake Away* and the fight to stop child hunger.